THE FABER EASY-PLAY KEYBOARD S

Play Romantic
Germany

FABER MUSIC

Contents

© 1989 by Faber Music Ltd
First published in 1989 by Faber Music Ltd
3 Queen Square, London WC1N 3AU
Music drawn by Sambo Music Engraving
Cover design and typography by John Bury
Printed in England

Sheep may safely graze

J.S. BACH

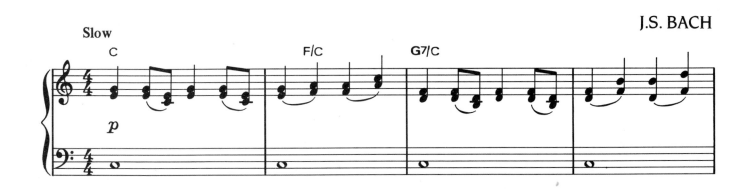

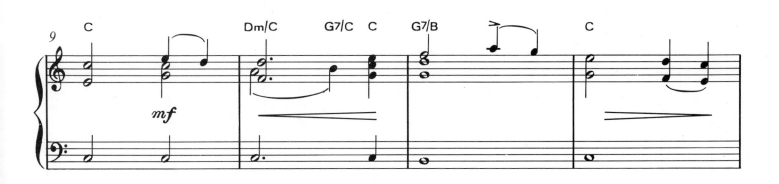

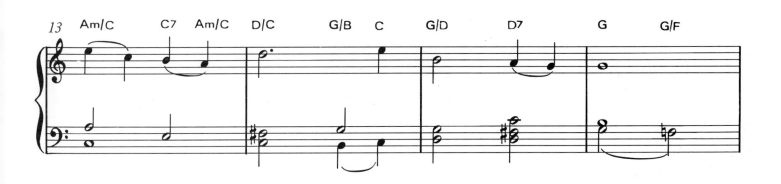

Air on the G string

J.S. BACH

Nocturne (A Midsummer Night's Dream)

FELIX MENDELSSOHN

Slow movement from Violin Concerto

FELIX MENDELSSOHN

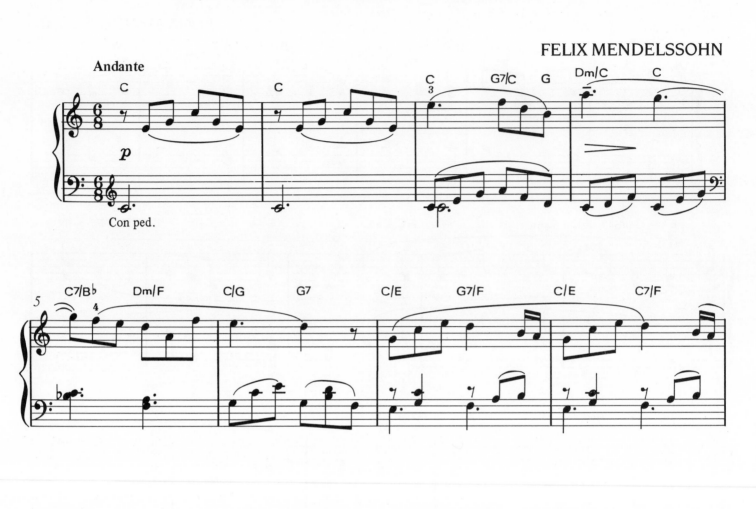

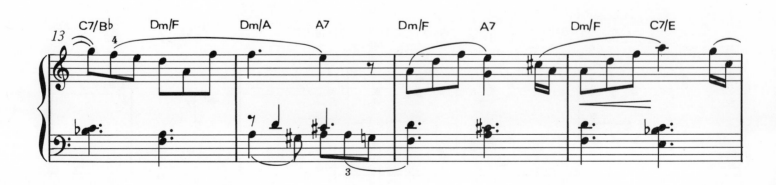

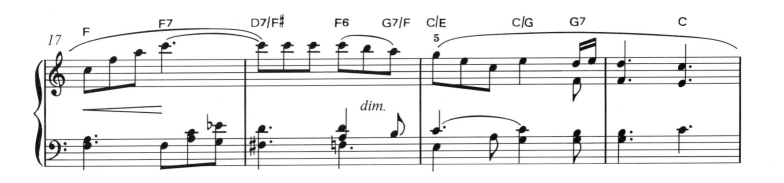

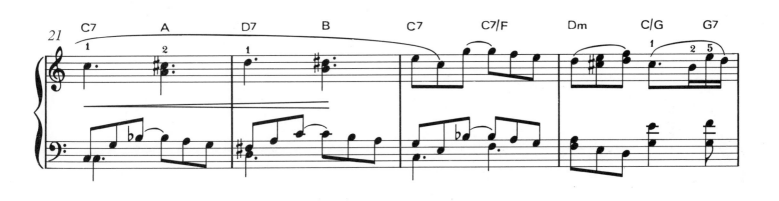

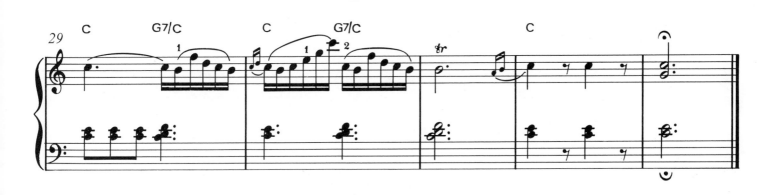

Wedding March (A Midsummer Night's Dream)

FELIX MENDELSSOHN

O for the wings of a dove

FELIX MENDELSSOHN

Theme from 'Italian' Symphony

FELIX MENDELSSOHN

Song without Words

FELIX MENDELSSOHN

On Wings of Song

FELIX MENDELSSOHN

Theme from Piano Concerto

ROBERT SCHUMANN

The Jolly Peasant

ROBERT SCHUMANN

Traumerei

ROBERT SCHUMANN

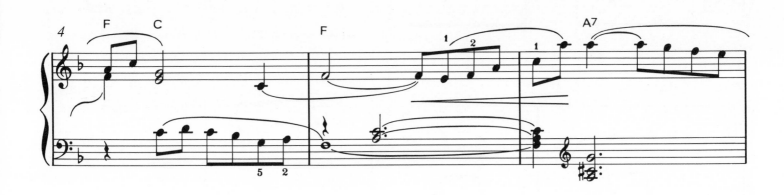

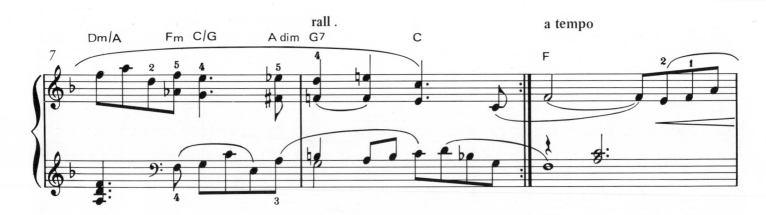

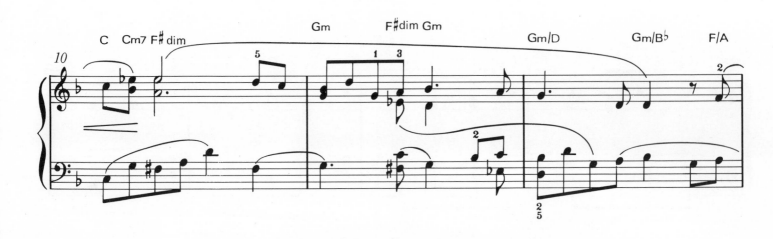

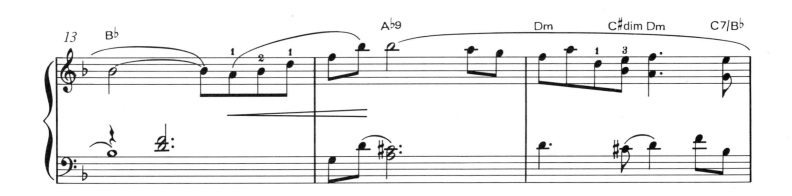

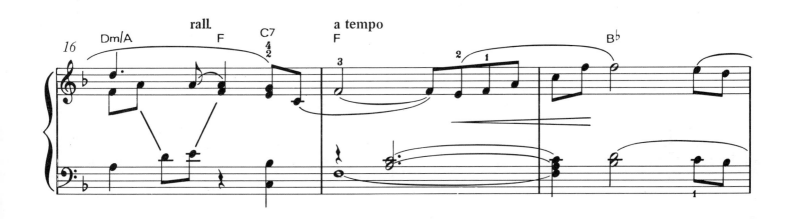

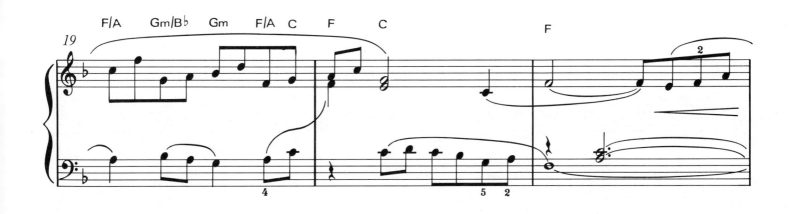

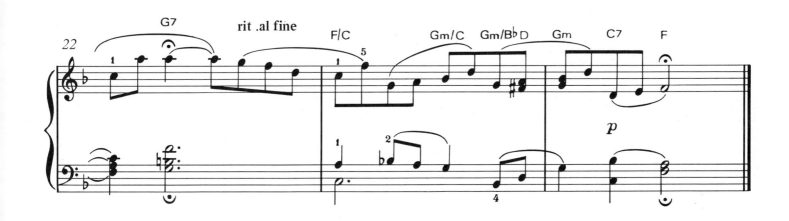

Theme from 'Rhenish' Symphony

ROBERT SCHUMANN

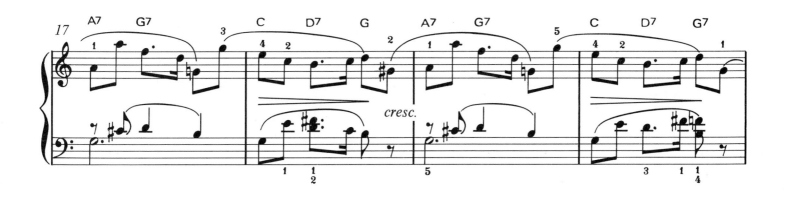

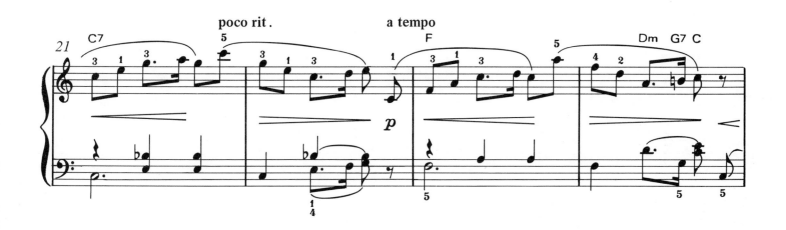

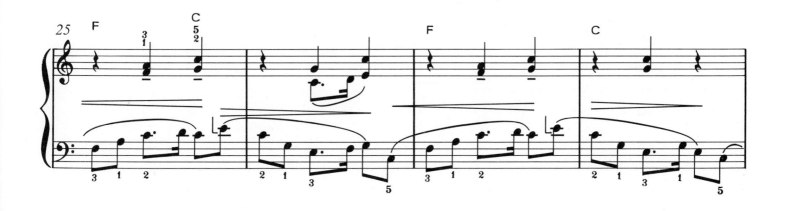

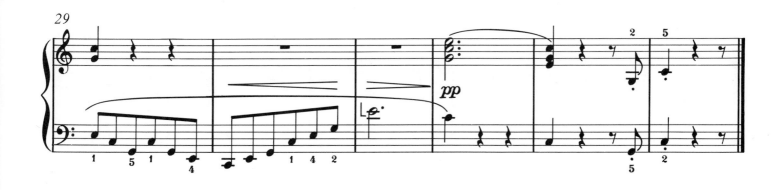

The Wild Horseman

ROBERT SCHUMANN

Soldiers' March

ROBERT SCHUMANN

Huntsmen's Chorus

CARL MARIA VON WEBER

Liebestraum

FRANZ LISZT

March (*The Mastersingers*)

RICHARD WAGNER

Liebestod (*Tristan and Isolde*)

RICHARD WAGNER

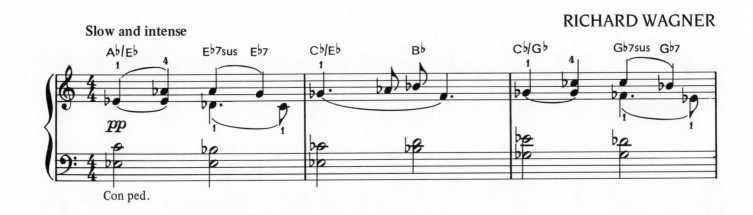

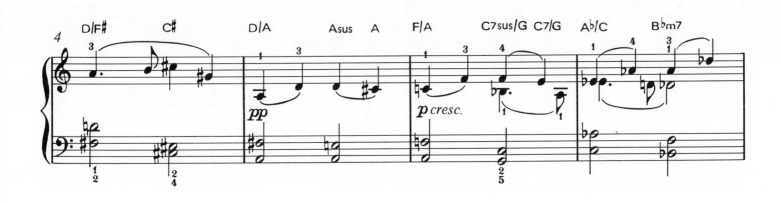

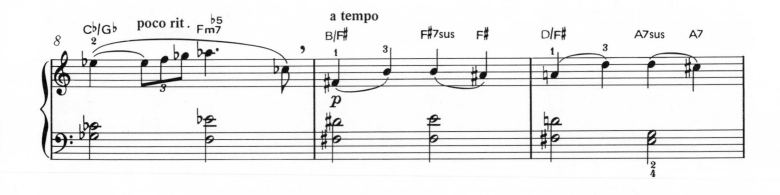

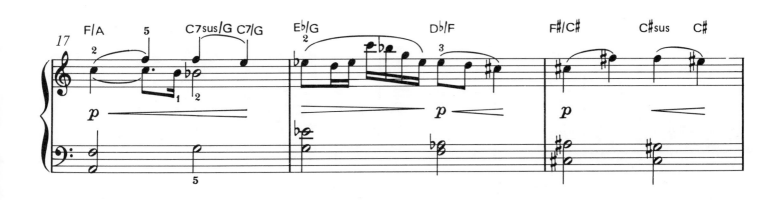

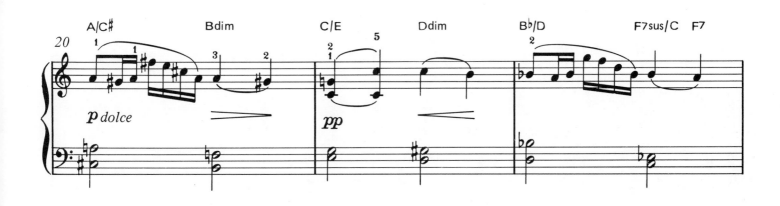

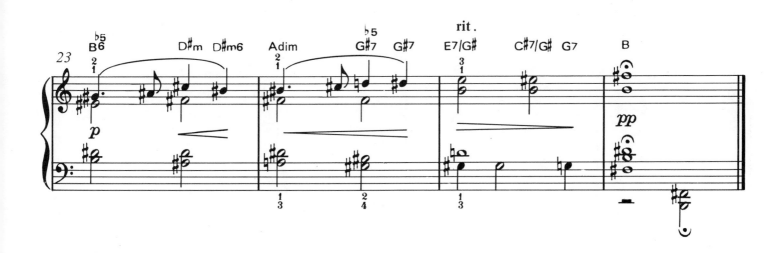

Bridal Chorus (*Lohengrin*)

RICHARD WAGNER

Prelude (*Lohengrin*)

RICHARD WAGNER

Ride of the Valkyries

RICHARD WAGNER

Pilgrim's Chorus (*Tannhäuser*)

RICHARD WAGNER